In Depth Guide to Price Action Trading

Powerful Swing Trading Strategy for Consistent Profits

By PA Traders

ISBN-10: 1539481654
ISBN-13: 978-1539481652

TABLE OF CONTENTS

OPENING WORDS

First of all, let me just say a few words about the design of this book you are about to read. It is meant to be a step by step guide with chart examples and explanations that teaches how to read price action movements, at the same time, formulating a clear trading plan with entry levels, stops and take profit targets. It will be as in depth and practical as a book can be, therefore, it is best to read it with a pen and paper. There will also be notes throughout the book after each component or concept is presented that suggests to open your trading charts and do some practice, then come back and continue reading.

The material presented assumes that you have

knowledge of basic market functionalities. Things like how to open a trade, what leverage to use and so forth will not be covered. If you are not yet familiar with these things you can get yourself up to speed in no time just by doing a simple online search. The book will focus only on what is really important in trading, that is what you can't find out with a simple online search. It is a material about technical analysis, about reading price movements and interpreting them in the best way possible. At the same time, as each chapter passes, a clear trading strategy with very sound price action logic and clear rules will take shape.

The material is for everyone interested in trading with price action and becoming a consistently successful and versatile trader. All that is presented will be explained thoroughly and logically. Technical analysis is applicable to stocks, indices, commodities, futures or any tradable instrument where the price is influenced by the forces of supply and demand. If you can trade it electronically by sitting in front of your computer and you can sell or buy instantly then that market is liquid enough. And where we have liquidity it means we will also have predictable price movements. Technical analysis will apply.

WHY USE PRICE ACTION?

Technical analysis or price action reading is the forecasting of future price movements based on an examination of past price movements. Like weather forecasting, technical analysis does not result in absolute predictions about the future. Instead, technical analysis can help investors anticipate what is "likely" to happen to prices over time. There are a number of reasons to choose trading with price action instead of indicators, robots, expert advisors and who knows what else.

It is much more efficient and much more rewarding. It will not clutter up your charts.

It is not market dependent. Once learned, you can use it to trade any liquid market you like. Price movements are nothing more than the outcome of buyer and seller behavior. And this behavior is the same in any market. It creates predictable movements over and over again. Unlike trading with indicators where some of them work in a market but fail in others.

Last but perhaps most important, learning to interpret price action movements will make a versatile trader out of you, able to adapt to the constantly changing market conditions. Trading by using technical indicators will not achieve that. That kind of trading approach suffers when the market condition is shifting from a trending environment to a non-trending one for example. Just keep this in mind: the best indicator that you can have to assist you in trading is your brain.

TIMEFRAMES

Okay, now that we got the introductory statements out of the way, it is time to get to the actual core of the book. The first thing you want to do is decide what type of trader you want to be. This is entirely up to you, your working schedule, your commitment to dedicate a certain amount of time to trading per day, your inclination and so forth. There are two types of traders. Swing traders and day traders. Swing trading is trading on higher timeframes like the 4 hours or daily, day trading is trading on lower timeframes such as the 15 minutes or 5 minute charts. There are even people who trade based on one minute charts, which is complete madness if you ask me. Mind as well go to the casino and through your money away.

I realize that everyone wants money, and they want it as fast as possible. Trading just doesn't work like that. Trading is a business that if done properly, will accumulate profits over time. It is not a get rich quick type of scheme. Especially beginner traders who are just starting out, feel compelled that in order for them to make money by trading they need to trade 10 times per day on the 5 minute charts while sitting in front of their computer the whole day. They lack patience and discipline, which are at the core of every successful trader, regardless of the trading strategy used. You can have the best trading plan at your disposal, if you are impatient, if you are not disciplined enough to follow it to the letter every single time, you will not come out as a successful trader.

Trading is simply a game of waiting for the best opportunities to present themselves. Think of it if you will, as a lion who waits patiently for a long time before making the move on its prey. If the lion is not disciplined, it will make its attack at the wrong time and the prey will escape.

Trading is not about the quantity of trades you can make per day, it is, and always will be, about the quality of those trades.

This being said, I recommend trading on higher timeframes for the following reasons:

It is easier to make money on a higher timeframe. The price action moves are not that erratic like on the lower timeframes. They are not subject to intraday market spikes, random moves or news that impact the lower timeframes on a daily basis.

The higher the timeframe, the more meaningful the price movements are. It is always best to have a bird's eye view of the market in order to make the best trading decisions possible. It is difficult to achieve this if you are trading on the 10 minute charts, subject to intraday trading noise and economic news.

Profits from trading are not made by trading 10 times per day on low timeframes. In fact, this is actually the recipe for losing your money. The trading volume, or the money you will put in each trade and risk management is what makes the profits. Ideally you should trade only 3-4 times per week, the best possible trading opportunities only. If there is a slow week, the market is not moving much, it is possible that it will not provide you with solid trading opportunities. There is absolutely no problem with that. Stay on the sidelines and wait for the next opportunity to trade. Resist the urge to go to lower timeframes and find trading setups. The sooner you embrace this fact, the faster you will become a consistently good trader. Only after you go on a lower timeframe and start losing your money you come to appreciate the real value of staying on the sidelines and waiting. Not doing anything is always better than losing.

I would recommend trading using the 4 hour charts. This

will not have you sitting in front of the computer the whole day, but it will make consistent profits month after month provided you follow your trading strategy to the letter. Trading based on price action from a higher timeframe like this one will ensure that you do not miss out on the bigger picture of price for that specific trading instrument. This is what the professional traders are doing, they don't make trading analysis based on the 5 minute intraday charts. It makes sense to follow them.

Picking the timeframe that will be used for analyzing price action movements is not complete if you do not take into account the next higher up timeframe. Remember about keeping an eye on the big picture. So, we will be using also the daily timeframe. This will be discussed later on.

Also, you will be needing to choose a lower timeframe than the 4 hours, to help you when it comes to locate the precise trade entry point. More on this later.

SUPPORT AND RESISTANCE ON HIGHER TIMEFRAME

If you haven't noticed, we have already started to build a solid trading plan, a logical one. The next logical step after deciding on the main timeframe you will be using to analyze price action and look for trading opportunities, is to go to the daily timeframe and find the support and resistance zones there. Remember that price action movements on higher timeframes always prevail over those on lower timeframes. They have more importance, more meaning because they took much more time to develop, they withstood the test of time more successfully than the movements on the lower timeframes like the 4 hours.

I am going to assume that not everybody reading this book is familiar with what support and resistance areas are and how to correctly identify them. For this reason, if you have some experience with support and resistance, if you are not completely new to trading, you can go ahead and skip this small section. Just as well, you can go ahead and read through, maybe you will find something that adds to your understanding of support and resistance areas.

A support or resistance is a zone or area where price is having a hard time pushing through it. The area is called resistance when it is above price and support when it is below price. Think of resistance as a ceiling and of support as a floor.

Support is the price level at which demand is thought to be strong enough to prevent the price from declining further. The logic dictates that as the price declines towards support and gets cheaper, buyers become more inclined to buy and sellers become less inclined to sell. By the time the price reaches the support level, it is believed that demand will overcome supply and prevent the price from falling below support.

Resistance is the price level at which selling is thought to be strong enough to prevent the price from rising further. The logic dictates that as the price advances towards resistance, sellers become more inclined to sell and buyers become less inclined to buy. By the time the price reaches the resistance level, it is believed that supply will overcome demand and prevent the price from rising above resistance.

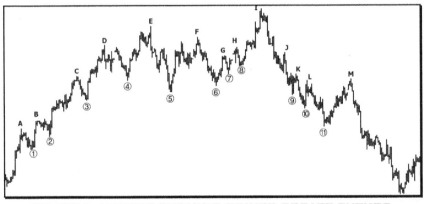

CHART 1: MARKET TURNING POINTS CREATE FUTURE SUPPORT AND RESISTANCE AREAS

This is a random chart. See the turning points or swings as they are called. A swing is nothing more than an area where price changes direction from up to down or vice versa. All those levels emphasized from 1 to 11 and from A to M are actually market swings or turning points, however you want to call them. Every time the market creates a swing, that is a possible future support or resistance zone in the making. Swings from I to II act as support for price and swings from A to M act as resistance.

If you strip down the price action movements further, these swings are actually the footprints of the buyers and sellers stepping into the market. I-II are the levels where buyers stepped into the market and pushed the price upwards. A-M are the price levels where sellers opened enough selling orders to create an imbalance in the order flow and push the price downwards. Everything in your price action analysis can be stripped down and reduced to the constant war between buyers and sellers. The chart you see above, along with its price swings, is the outcome of the battle between the two sides.

Now back to support and resistance areas. The swings

above are only just minor support and resistance levels. This is how the areas take shape. Each of those single swings can be revisited by price once or more times in the future, adding strength to it and developing an area of support or resistance for price. We are looking for zones of support or areas. This means that one single swing is not enough to consider it an area. We need at least two to join with a straight line in order to form a support or resistance area.

Look at swing 4 for example in the chart above. Price revisited that level again with swing 6. This gives you the opportunity to draw a straight horizontal line joining 4 and 6 swings and calling it a support area for price. Also, swing 5 happened in roughly the same price area. It is safe to include this one too and consider it as a revisit of swing 4. The word "area" is key. Think of these lines that you will be drawing on the charts as areas and not as exact levels of price. The 5 swing doesn't happen exactly at the same price level as 4 and 6 but it does happen in close proximity or, in the area around them.

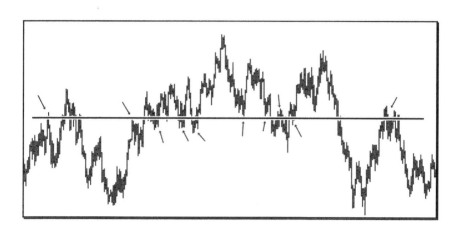

CHART 2 : PIVOTAL SUPPORT AND RESISTANCE ZONE

This chart above shows what will you be looking for on the daily chart to mark, prior to doing your price action analysis on the 4h timeframe. This line on the above chart can be a strong resistance if current price is below it and an equally powerful support if price is above it. As opposed to the first example where you see 3 swings in the same area (swings 4,5 and 6), in this chart you can see price making swings on both sides of the line. This behavior is what makes the horizontal line act as a pivot for price. The pivotal nature gives it extra strength. The area takes turns in being both support and resistance for price.

See how price is making turning points in this area where the line is plotted. Both from below and above it. Considering this is a daily timeframe and every single bar in this chart represents a whole day of trading, notice how much time price has spent respecting this area of price over the years. It finds it very tough to break through this area in either direction. The swings that shape this powerful pivotal support and resistance area are emphasized with arrows on the chart if you haven't noticed this already. See how some of these swings above or below the line, do not align perfectly with it. This is normal, as said above, you need to consider this as an area where price will find it hard getting through it and not an exact level of price.

When drawing support and resistance on the daily chart you need to look carefully and see areas where price has made swings. It is not hard. It will come with practice if you are not accustomed.

WHAT PURPOSE DOES THIS SERVE?

The reason you need to draw support and resistance on the next higher timeframe than the one you will be doing your analysis on, should be obvious enough. It will help keeping a bird's eye view on the market at all times. In turn, this will keep you out of potentially losing trades. Take the chart above for example. Whenever price comes from below to hit the horizontal line, it makes a swing, it changes direction. If you wouldn't have taken the daily resistance into account and just started looking for trading setups on the 4h chart you would have registered some losses in this area just below the line. You would have bought only for price to reverse direction on you, causing losses. Apart from losses, it would have made you start questioning your own trading strategy.

The same would have happened in the other direction. If

you would have sold when price made those swings above the line, you would have suffered additional losses.

Context is the key word to remember, to keep in the back of your head every time you are doing your analysis. Time frames are related to each other, price movements on the higher ones always impact the movements on the lower ones. Put everything into the proper context. Higher timeframes price movements always prevail over those from the lower ones.

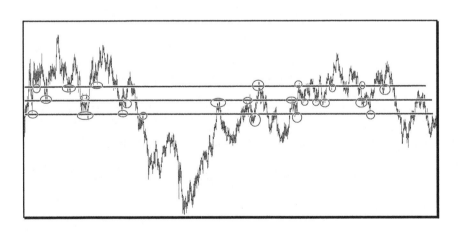

CHART 3 : SUPPORT AND RESISTANCE SUBJECTIVITY

Above you can see another example of support and

resistance area that you should identify and mark on the daily chart. I have plotted 3 lines instead of one to point out the subjectivity involved when it comes to identifying such areas.

Each one of these 3 lines is a pivotal support and resistance area for price. Each one has swings above and below it. Each one acts as a barrier for price, causing it to change direction often. The little circles are the price swings that formed each horizontal line. Would you have drawn these lines exactly the same as I did? No. In fact, if I delete the lines from the chart and start over, the chances are that I will not be able to draw the exact same 3 lines again, at the exact same price levels.

WHY? Because of the abundance of swings all over the place in that area. It almost seems like if you were to close your eyes and draw a horizontal line randomly in that area, the chances are, there are enough swings piercing it from above and below to consider it a valid support and resistance area. These are clusters of pivotal support and resistance levels. You will encounter this situation often. If you are undecided as to which line you should take into account or which has the most swings on both sides of it just do what I did in the above chart. Do not start to count the price swings of each line as this should not be a mathematical approach. Draw all the lines that you think are relevant, that you feel qualify for being labeled as a support or resistance for price. The zone from the lower line to the higher one will be your support and resistance area that you will be taking into account on the 4h chart to act as a filter for bad trades. You wouldn't want to be buying straight into the area shown in the above chart.

There is no right or wrong line, the important thing is to identify the area and estimate its boundaries. These areas where you can find multiple support and resistance levels are especially powerful in rejecting price and causing it to change direction. The more lines you can find in a relatively tight area of price like the one in the above chart, the more impact the area will have on the price movements from the lower timeframe such as the 4h.

Before you go on reading the next section, I suggest you take some time and get more familiar with what has been presented so far. It will help your understanding of the upcoming sections of the book.

Open your trading platform.

Go to the daily charts and try to find a resistance and a support area for current price.

Look closely, find the price swings, join as many as you can with a horizontal line.

Don't seek ideal lines where all swings align perfectly. This rarely happens. It is perfectly okay to have some of the swings pierce quickly through the line and then bounce off of it.

Try to find clusters of support and resistance as discussed above. Embrace the subjectivity of drawing these lines. There is no wrong line.

Draw your own conclusions.

ESTABLISH TREND

Okay, so you have identified the important support and resistance zones above and below where current price is. You are ready now to go to the 4h charts and start your price action analysis. The first thing you need to do is to put some order into all the chaos. You need to find out what the trend is. All trades will be placed only in the direction of this overall trend. The reason for this is that the probability of making a successful trade going with the trend is much higher than if you are entering the market against the main trend. This is what trading is, a game of probabilities.

Simply put, a financial security is trending upwards when there are more buying orders in the market than there are selling orders. Conversely when the trend is pointing downwards. When I say more buying or selling orders I don't mean the exact number of orders. I mean the size or volume of all orders entered into the market in the same direction. This is what creates the price action movements you see on any chart. The imbalance between total volume of buying orders and total volume of selling orders.

There are 3 ways to find out what the current trend is. It is best that you learn them all and combine them in your analysis. If all 3 say the same thing, then you will have great confidence in placing a trade in the trend's direction.

SWINGS

The first one is looking at the price swings.

CHART 4 : PRICE SWINGS BECOME HIGHS AND LOWS

Notice in this chart how price is making swings, every time at a lower price area than the preceding one. Think of these turning points or swings as waves if you want. This is a downtrend as price is making successive lower highs (LH) and successive lower lows (LL). This means that you will be looking to sell only. In fact, this is the definition of a price action downtrend. Price will always make lower highs and lower lows. When it stops making them, there are 2 possibilities. The market will start moving sideways (the trend is neutral) or the trend will change direction.

On this same chart you can see a failed attempt to turn the downtrend into an uptrend. On the right side of the chart, the move up makes a higher high (HH). That is a higher high because it goes up above the last LH of the downtrend. You will see many of these failed attempts on your charts, the important thing is to learn to acknowledge them as such and not be tricked into thinking the trend has changed direction.

As a general rule, the downtrend will end and an uptrend will emerge only after the new higher low (HL) will be confirmed by subsequent price action. Subsequent price action translates into a move upwards that will surpass the new HH. This is illustrated by the diagonal arrow pointing upwards on the chart. Only when that up move happens and price goes past the area of the HH you can consider that the downtrend has ended and a new uptrend has begun. In this case, the upwards move past the HH did not happen so there is no confirmation that the trend has changed. You are still looking to sell at this point. For a downtrend to change into an uptrend you need a confirmed HL.

CHART 5 : TREND CHANGE BEHAVIOR

Okay, this chart is full of notes. It looks pretty intimidating but it will help for a better understanding of how analyzing high and lows provides valuable clues and improves your overall trading.

On the left side of the chart you see a clear uptrend as price is making consecutive higher highs(HH) and higher lows(HL). It makes 4 such pairs of HH-HL. On the 5th try you can see price making another HH but failing with a new HL. Price goes below the last HL of the uptrend, making a lower low (LL). At this point in time, even if the uptrend is giving signs that it might end, you do not have a confirmation of that, so you are looking to buy. The confirmation that the trend is now pointing downwards comes with the down move below the LL, that I have market as "1" on the chart, the one with a down pointing arrow alongside it. The double headed arrow above it is there so you can see the comparison between the last HH of the uptrend and the first HL of the downtrend. Only after the "1" move goes below past the LL you can conclude that a downtrend has started and look to sell from there on.

Moving on, the downtrend is short lived as you can see, it can only manage to print 2 pairs of LH-LL's and another LL right there at the bottom. It then prints a HH (pointed out on the chart by the double headed arrow). Again, a simple HH is not sufficient to conclude that the trend has now changed again. You are still looking to sell at this point. There are a lot of false trend changes as you've seen in the preceding example and will see on this very chart momentarily. You need that HH confirmed by a price move up, past it. The move comes. It is the "2" move on the chart. It goes above the HH, confirming the first HL of the new uptrend. Only when the "2" move goes above HH you can conclude that the trend has changed once again and start looking to buy.

Moving on once more, the uptrend doesn't last very long, it manages to print 3 pairs of HH-HL's and fails to print a new HH (emphasized on the chart with the "NO HH" label). Price moves down below the last HL of the uptrend. Once again, you need to wait for the confirmation move that the uptrend has ended. And this is where it becomes interesting.

After the LL, price goes back up and then starts a down move that would normally be the confirmation move going below the LL that you are waiting for to conclude that you now have a downtrend in place. This confirmation move is, however, long awaited as you can see. There are not one but 2 failed confirmation attempts there. I am talking about "3" and "4" marked out on the chart. Neither of those moves succeed in going below the LL, confirming change of trend. All this time where price tries to go down below LL but can't, you are still looking to buy. For what you are concerned, until proven otherwise, the trend is still up and price can shoot back up making new HH's at any time. And it will do just this often times, after such failure attempts to change the trend.

In this particular case it didn't however. It made a 3rd attempt to go past the LL and it succeeded this time. I agree that this method of judging the trend can prove a bit complicated sometimes but it is the most rewarding, as you will find out. It will improve your trading, it is worth the time put into it, there is no doubt about it. It has been used for a long time in trading. Done correctly, it will never let you down, with some practice it will become second nature.

CHART 6: SIDEWAYS MOVEMENT. NON TRENDING ENVIRONMENT

When doing your highs and lows analysis, make sure that you always pay attention to context. See the price movements in this chart, engulfed in that rectangle. Price seems to be making swings there, there could be highs and lows. The problem is that all that price area is completely engulfed by the last LH-LL pair. You will be marking a new HH only when the LH on the left is broken above. You will be marking a LL only when the last LL will be broken below. If neither of these situations occur (just as it happened in the box above) you do not mark anything as the market is moving sideways. There is no clear trend, the buyers and sellers are in agreement to keep the price at this level. You are not looking to buy and you are not looking to sell as long as price stays in the rectangle. You move on to another security to analyze and trade.

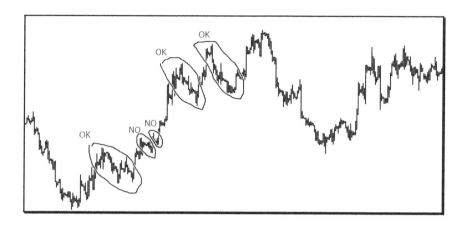

CHART 7: SIZE MATTERS

Another thing that you need to be aware of is not to mix apples with cherries so to speak. When marking high and lows you will find swings or waves (like those marked on the chart) of different sizes. You need to mark with highs and lows only the waves of roughly the same size. In this case, the first one and the last 2. Again, this is not mathematical. When you see very small waves, that do not resemble in size in any way, the preceding ones, you should skip them. Do not mark them with highs and lows. They are of a different degree. They are relevant to a smaller timeframe only. On the 4h timeframe they do not hold much importance to the overall trend. I am talking of course about waves such as those market with "NO" on the chart.

Feel free to take a break from reading now and go on to your trading platform once again.

Find the trends, see what happens when the trend changes direction.

See how many false trend changes there are and what happens after each. Get accustomed to this type of price behavior.

Analyze highs and lows until you get familiar with them.

Put everything into the proper context, notice the sideways movements and how they create highs and lows inside bigger highs and lows.

Notice how many waves of smaller degree there are within those of the proper size. Analyze how marking these tiny waves would have affected your goal to judge the trend properly.

CONGESTION AREAS

Another extremely useful tool when trying to identify the overall price action trend is to notice the congestion areas that price makes and the direction of their movement. A congestion area is simply an area where price spends enough time moving back and forth, confined within relatively the same price area. Usually these areas are created when the main trend is taking a breath and price is going sideways for a while. Congestion areas can also take place when a retracement move happens, opposite to the trend's direction. It starts as a simple counter trend move but then price spends quite some time in the area making small swings.

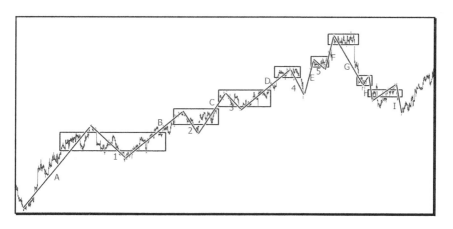

CHART 8: CONGESTION AREAS

In the above chart you can see areas marked with rectangles. Those are congestion areas that price makes on its way up. You can clearly see that there is an uptrend in place as the market is making easily identifiable higher highs and higher lows. However, you can further strengthen your belief by noticing these congestion areas movement direction. As with the price swings, these areas too happen every time at a higher and higher price area. On the chart you can see I drew lines on top of price to make the uptrend even more obvious. The longer diagonal lines, pointing upwards, in line with the uptrend (those marked from A to I) are impulsive moves, created by the buyers stepping into the market with force and pushing price up, convinced that the price of this security should be higher.

The shorter diagonal lines (marked from 1-5) are the retracement moves of the uptrend. Price is moving counter the trend because those buyers are closing some of their positions, are marking their profits. This is how a healthy trend looks like and these are the ones you will be looking for to trade. What you see in this chart is normal price behavior. We are looking to trade and speculate on this normal, predictable price behavior. I've only marked the retracement moves up to 5 so not to clutter up the chart. As you can see, after impulsive move F, price does not make a small retracement move to accompany the impulsive one. It makes another impulsive move pointing downwards (move G) that goes below the start of the impulsive move F.

In these retracement moves against the direction of the main trend is where congestion areas are formed. Price is moving slowly as there aren't enough sellers, and the buyers, after marking some profits, are waiting for price to go lower in order to buy again. This is the constant battle between buyers and sellers. Every side wants to enter into the market at an advantageous price level. Sellers want to sell higher and buyers want to buy lower.

In each of these congestion areas you can see price is

basically non directional. It spends time in the same price areas, back and forth, printing small swings inside other swings. Even without drawing rectangles on the chart you can see with the naked eye that these congestion areas take place higher and higher every time. This is an indication that you are looking at an uptrend.

Notice what happens after the impulsive move G, counter the trend. Price is now making congestion areas at lower price levels. As with price failing to make a new higher low and printing a new lower high, this too is an indication that maybe we are seeing the trend change direction.

You can also see that this did not happen eventually. The uptrend resumed. Have you any idea why? We discussed earlier in the swings section that the size of the swings matter and everything has to be analyzed in the surrounding context. The size of the congestion areas matters too. See how the first 3 rectangles are roughly in the same size area. The next 3 are very small. Price hits a top, goes in a retracement all the way to the 3rd congestion area of the uptrend, finds support there and resumes the trend.

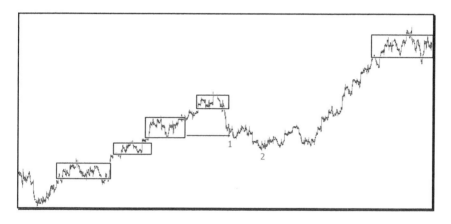

CHART 9: JUDGE TREND CHANGE WITH CONGESTION AREAS

As with the first chart, here we also have an uptrend. Price is making highs and lows. I have not marked them as they should be obvious. Also they will clutter up the chart. I did mark with rectangles the congestion areas. They are saying the same thing as the swings. The trend is up.

After the 4th congestion area, price goes to make a retracement counter the main uptrend. See how the previous congestion area provides support for price at point 1. There are times when marking the congestions areas, helps to see a trend change or a trend change failure faster and clearer than by marking highs and lows. As with swings, the rule of a trend change, congestion areas wise, is that we need confirmation. The confirmation would be a new congestion area of roughly the same size as the others, happening below the 3rd one of the uptrend.

If we would have analyzed this chart by marking the price swings, we would have seen that the forth pair of HH-HL (the 4th congestion area- rectangle) is of a smaller size or degree than the previous ones. The same with the congestion area analysis. The 4th rectangle is not in the same size area as the others.

You can see that price find strong support at point 1,

goes shortly below making a very small congestion area (marked with 2), only to come back up quickly and stay there. If that would have been a big enough congestion area at point 2, you would have had the confirmation that the uptrend has ended. This, as with the swings, would have sent you on the lookout for selling trade setups from there on. The support area at point 1 that the 3rd congestion area offers is where all the buying orders are located as you can see. Price makes a very strong, very large up move from there on.

This is another characteristic of the congestion areas that we will make use of. They provide reliable support and resistance areas. They act as a barrier for price. One important concept that we will be using is the fact that these congestion areas are very territorial. Besides horizontal support areas as with the example above, they also provide diagonal support or resistance areas for future price movements.

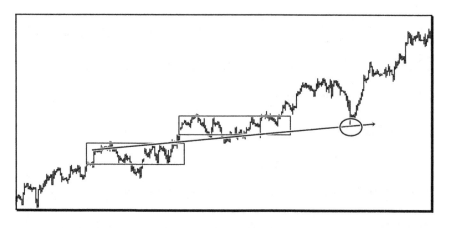

CHART 10 : DIAGONAL SUPPORT FOR FUTURE PRICE

This is another uptrend, as normal as it can be. Several pairs of HH-HL's, several congestion areas, each at a higher price area than the previous. I have marked the first 2 congestion areas with rectangles to show exactly how useful they are in providing future support areas for price. The diagonal line that you see on the chart pointing upwards is made simply by joining the upper limit of the first congestion area with the lower limit of the second one. I have extended the line to show how future price action reacted to it.

Price obviously found strong support right at the line, in the circled area. This technique will be used later on in the book when we try to find the confluence area, the area where all winning trades have the most chances to happen. The trend is up in this situation so the diagonal support (extended line) has to be pointing upwards as well.

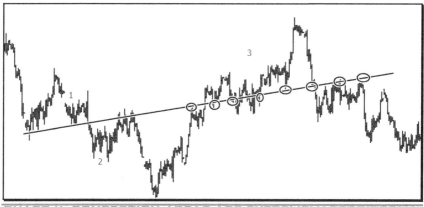

CHART 11: CONGESTION AREAS ARE EXTREMELY TERRITORIAL

See this chart above. On the left side of it there is a downtrend in place. You can see the 1 and 2 congestion areas. If, as with the first example, you join with a simple line the bottom of the congestion area 1 with the top of the congestion area 2, what you get is a very powerful pivotal support and resistance area for future price. The space above the line is territory of congestion area 1 and the space below is the territory of congestion area 2.

Notice that the line is pointing counter the downtrend so we couldn't use it when looking for potential selling trade setups in that downtrend. However, even when price goes above congestion area 2 and stays there (making you think that the trend has changed direction. See big congestion area 3), the line proves a strong barrier for price coming from both above and below it. This shows how territorial these congestion areas can be and how much help can they provide in trading, when trying to find future support and resistance for price. As said before, this concept will be incorporated in the next section of the book.

Its time now for another break from reading. Please go to the charts on your trading platform once again and get familiar with congestion areas.

On the same charts where you did the practice with the highs and lows, go ahead and mark the congestion areas now. See if both types of analysis arrive to the same exact conclusion.

Go to the areas where you have identified a change of trend using the highs-lows method and see what happened there, congestion areas wise. See if both types of analysis agree that there is indeed a change of trend there.

Notice the different sizes of the congestion areas and see how taking into account an "out of context" congestion area would have hurt you trend analysis conclusions.

Try to find future support areas by joining, in an uptrend, the upper boundary of any congestion area with the lower boundary of the next one of in the same size area. You should get an extended diagonal line pointing upwards. Notice how future price reacts to it.

In a downtrend, join the lower boundary of any random congestion area, with the next immediate one of roughly the same size, in the same downtrend. You should get an extended diagonal line pointing downwards. See how future price reacts to that line's extension.

BIG DIRECTIONAL BARS/CANDLES

A third way of judging the current main trend's direction is by looking at big bars or candles that price makes. This is of course a complementary type of quick analysis that you can do with your naked eye. It should not be used alone when finding out the trend. It should serve as confirmation and enforcement for the swings and congestion areas methods of analyzing the trend.

CHART 12: DIRECTIONAL CANDLES SHOWING THE DOWNTREND

I have chosen a candlestick chart because it makes it easier to see this price behavior. This is a downtrend, judging either by marking highs and lows or observing congestion areas. A directional candle is one with no or very small lower wick if it's pointing downwards. A big directional candle is one that you notice right away with a simple glimpse on the chart. A candle of a bigger length then the one/ones on its left. A candle that looks like it doesn't belong there, in its surroundings.

The arrows on the chart point to big directional candles in this downtrend. "Directional" means that they have a big body and no or very small lower wick. "Big", as said, means big when put into context, when compared with the most recent candles on its left. All these candles in the above chart confirm that there is indeed a downtrend. Counter the trend, you can see only small white candles where, in line with the downtrend, you can see periodically a big directional candle.

WHAT DO THEY MEAN?

The chart above is a 4h's one. Simply put, these directional big candles show the footprint of money or trading volume entering the market. To make an idea of their meaning, you must take the time component into consideration. Every single one of those candles in the chart represent four hours of trading time. Let's take the last big directional candle on the right end of the chart for example. Notice how, just on the left side of it (engulfed by the rectangle), price is moving sideways, printing small white or black candles. Each of those show 4 hours of trading so there must be about 2 days of trading incorporated into those tiny indecisive candles. The candle that comes after them, resuming the downtrend, represents only 4 hours of trading. In other words, price has moved in 4 hours, much more than it moved in 2 days of trading. There is only one thing that could have caused this. Increased supply in the area, or a lot of selling orders entered into the market at that area. This shows where the traders with big trading volumes enter the market.

CHART 13: BIG DIRECTIONAL BARS SIGNALING UPTREND

The same with an uptrend, we see big white directional candles that show the footprint of buyers entering into the market. Often times, the area where the big candle moves away from the surrounding candles on its left will provide support or resistance for future price.

Beware that you will not always find such candles. That is perfectly okay, but when they do show up on your charts you now know their meaning and importance. They show money entering the market and they provide support or resistance for price often times.

Please go to the same practice charts once again on your trading platform and try to find these directional candles in both uptrends and downtrends. See the correlation between them and the other types of trends analysis.

Observe if the area where the big directional candle moves away from surrounding candles provides a small support or resistance for future price movements.

LOOK FOR THE HEALTHY TRENDS ONLY

This is to say that when scanning through you preferred stocks, forex pairs, commodities, to find trading setups you need to pick only the ones with healthy trends. These trends do respect technical analysis the most. You will have the most chances of success when trading these trends. A healthy trend is every trend shown as an example in this book so far. It should have high-low pairs of relatively the same size, should have congestion areas, should have impulsive moves in the direction of the trend, followed by smaller, retracement moves, in the opposite direction of the trend. A not so healthy trend is one where the price movements have been severely influenced by big impact fundamental news, changing trader's behavior and making it extremely unpredictable.

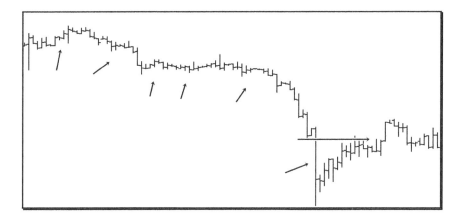

CHART 14: NON HEALTHY TREND.

See this chart. Price is slowly moving downwards but there are no clear highs and lows, no clear congestion areas. Only small candles that moves very slowly to the downside. No clear impulsive down moves, no clear retracement moves against the trend. To make it even worse, there is a huge bar pushing the price down at the last arrow there which was surely generated by strong fundamental news coming out that made people behave in this unpredictable manner. That move is not the result of the war between buyers and seller. It is a complete sell off. The buyers are nowhere to be seen.

The idea is that you need predictability. You need predictable moves in the market in order to make successful trades. This type of erratic price movements and trends without the characteristics of a normal trend, you will have to move away from.

As a side note, see that horizontal arrow. The big directional down move created small resistance for future price in the area where it moved away from the surrounding price action. When you see a big move like that and price comes back in the area where it left the surrounding price, you can be sure it will bounce off of that area for a little while, it will not go through it like a knife through butter.

CONFLUENCE ZONE

This section of the book introduces what I like to call a confluence area. This is the area where you will look for setups after identifying the trend.

So far, you have decided on what timeframes to use, have plotted support and resistance areas above and below the current price and identified the trend direction. Knowing how one specific trading instrument is trending is not enough though. You can't just enter trades randomly in the direction of the trend and expect to become profitable on a consistent basis. You need an area inside the trend where you will wait for price to reach in order to enter the market in the trend's direction. Remember that a good trader always looks to buy lower and sell higher. This type of trading approach ensures that you are minimizing risk and maximizing profits. At the beginning of the book I said that you will be only taking trades with a very high probability of success. Well, the vast majority of such trades are found in this confluence area inside the trend.

In a trend, buying lower and selling higher basically means that you need to wait for a retracement move or a countertrend move such as those we've discussed. These are the small, opposite to the trend's direction moves, where traders are closing some of their positions in order to mark profits. Revisit chart 8 once again to see the impulsive moves and retracement moves of a trend.

First of all, let me explain what confluence is. In trading, the more reasons the market gives you to buy or sell, the better it is. The greater the chances are for that trade to become a winner. There are millions of traders out there, each with their own strategy, each with their understanding of the market. You already know that you need to go with the trading volume in order to come out as a winner.

Some people buy the market because they see price has touched a support area and bounced, some buy because they see a rejected Fibonacci retracement level, which is just another type of support. Some buy because they see a bullish price pattern or a bullish candlestick pattern. In order to enter a high probability winning trade, you need to buy in the area where there are the greatest chances that all of the above and more, will be encountered, an area of price where it is most likely that you will find the support level, the Fibonacci level, a price pattern and more, cramped up inside it.

This is a confluence of factors, a confluence of buying signals, all cramped inside a small price area, at the end of the retracement move of a trend.

DEVELOP THE CONFLUENCE AREA

We are going to use 2 lines that will define the confluence area's limits or boundaries. You will be expecting price to go down and revisit the area inside these lines in an uptrend. Conversely, you will be expecting price to go back up and revisit the area delimited by the 2 lines in a downtrend.

These lines are in fact support and resistance levels derived from price movements. In an uptrend, the lines will take the shape of an ascending triangle. In a downtrend, they will resemble a descending triangle.

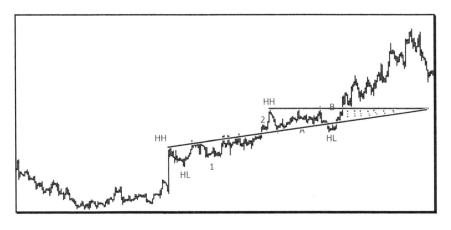

CHART 15: CONFLUENCE AREA IN AN UPTREND

This is how the confluence area looks like in an uptrend. I have marked the HH-HL pairs, the 1 and 2 are the congestion areas. The A line is the lower line of the confluence area. Go back to the congestion areas section of the book and see where we discussed about the territorial nature of these. Line A is the territorial separation between congestion area 1 and 2. Identical to those shown in chart 10 and chart 11. As said there, joining the upper side of the first congestion area with the lower side of the next congestion area provides a diagonal support for future price. This is what Line A is.

Line B is simply the extension of the last HH of the uptrend which also now constitutes a support area for price coming from above. All of this analysis, made with the consideration in mind that the current price is above congestion area 2 and is now moving down, towards our confluence area.

In an uptrend, line A has to be pointing up, just like the one in the above chart. Line B will always be a horizontal one.

The area between these lines, where the double headed arrows are, is the confluence area where you are expecting price to revisit in order to start looking for a setup to buy.

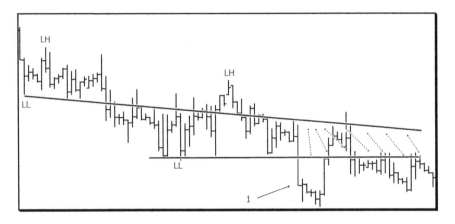

CHART 16: CONFLUENCE AREA IN A DOWNTREND

This is a clear downtrend as you can see. Price is making lower highs and lower lows, the congestion areas are visible, one below the other. The upper, diagonal descending line is the territorial resistance between the two congestion areas. The horizontal line is the extension of the last LL of the downtrend. Together they help develop the confluence area emphasized by those dotted arrows. The "1" area marked on the chart with the simple arrow below there, is where current price would

IN DEPTH GUIDE TO PRICE ACTION TRADING

be when you are developing the confluence area.

FIBONACCI RETRACEMENTS

So you have 2 support or resistance areas that make up the confluence area. These will likely stop the price and resume the main trend. The fact is, you have another support or resistance in that area but you don't see it on the chart. It is called a Fibonacci retracement level.

Unlike the 2 lines of support and resistance that are derived from raw price action, the Fibonacci retracement levels are derived mathematically. They work very well in providing support and resistance for price. The most effective is by far the 50% retracement level, followed by the 61.8%.

These retracement levels are simply a measurement of the last impulsive move of the trend to see how much of it (percentage wise) price has retraced. The 50%

retracement level simply means that price has gone counter the trend half of its last impulsive move.

In an uptrend like that on chart 15, the 50% or the 61.8% or both retracement levels are calculated by plotting the Fibonacci retracements tool on the last impulsive move of the uptrend which starts at the last HL and ends all the way to the top when price begins to retrace. This Fibonacci retracements tool can be found in just about every trading platform out there. You do not necessarily need to draw it on your charts, this is just to make you aware that most of the times, one of these retracement levels or both will be found there, inside your determined confluence area, further acting as a barrier for price. This increases even more the changes for the trend to resume.

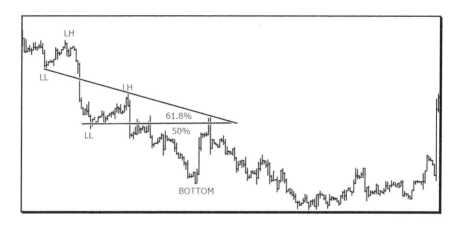

CHART 17: FIB LEVELS INSIDE OR NEAR THE CONFLUENCE AREA

In a downtrend, the Fibonacci retracement levels are measured based on the length of the last impulsive move of the downtrend. It starts from the last LH of the chart above and it ends where it says bottom, where price starts to retrace. "LH" to "Bottom" is the last impulsive move of the downtrend. You can see the confluence area delimited by the descending triangle and you can see price going up back inside it only to later resume the downtrend. This is what your selling trade will look like. You will sell in the confluence area where price has retraced and take profit when price goes all the way down to bottom. But more on this in upcoming sections.

Notice how one retracement level is situated at the base of the confluence area and the other one is actually inside it. Again, you do not need to measure these levels. It will only clutter up your charts. Just know that they will be present there in the majority of trades you will be making, acting as further barrier for price and giving you one more reason to enter a trade on the chance that the trend will resume. It gives you more confidence when trading, knowing there is one extra support or resistance for price there.

WHY DO YOU NEED THIS CONFLUENCE AREA?

We've discussed throughout the book about taking trades with the highest probability of success. Sure, you could see wining trades even if the setup does not happen inside the confluence area. You could and you will. But are these trades winners consistently? Definitely not.

The confluence area, as it was described above, has 3 or

4 support and resistance zones for price. If the trend is going to resume, this is the area where it has the greatest chances of doing so. There are 3-4 barriers there, each with orders ready to get triggered and reverse the direction of price.

The confluence area, because it is packed with support and resistance zones, it has the greatest concentration of pending orders in the direction of the trend. If one good trader wants to bet on the resumption of the main trend after a small correction, he will most likely put his pending order inside this confluence area.

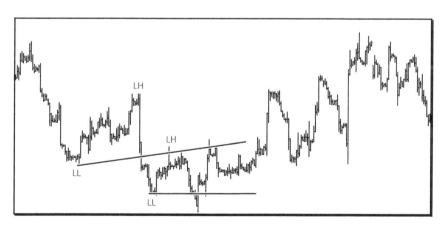

CHART 18: THERE IS NO TRIANGLE TO MAKE A VALID CONFLUENCE AREA

See this downtrend. Price is making LH-LL pairs, congestion areas moving lower. However, when you join the bottom of 1st congestion area with the top of the 2nd one you get a diagonal line pointing against the trend. Together with the horizontal line they definitely to not take the shape of a descending triangle as they should.

It simply means that there will be no trade setup there and you have to move away and look somewhere else. Most likely the downtrend is ending and the waves of the trend are happening very close to each other. The impulsive LH-LL moves of the downtrend are short. You will encounter from time to time, situations like these where the trends are approaching termination. The diagonal territorial line pointing against the trend would be yet another signal that the trend is about to end.

Please take some time off from reading now and go to your charts again.

Look at uptrends, look at downtrends and find the confluence area each time the trend is in retracement mode. Notice how many there are per each trend and how many times the trend resumes beginning from inside the confluence area.

Draw your own conclusions

Practice with the lines, see what happens when the diagonal line is at a much steeper angle than the ones shown in the above examples. For a healthy trend, the diagonal line part of the confluence area should be, well, diagonal, more or less.

If it tends to become almost horizontally, that is not good as the retracement move would have to be very big in order for price to revisit the confluence area. A lengthy retracement like that could go all the way surpassing the last HL or the last LH, putting the whole trend in question and hitting your stop loss level.

If the line that you get by joining the congestion areas tends to become steeper, almost vertical, that is not good either. It's just not practical as the retracement would have to be very small for price to touch the confluence area and resume the trend. In this case you take on the risk to have get your stops hit as well. A deeper retracement, past your confluence area would be expected.

Study these situations on your charts and take notes, draw your own conclusions.

A healthy trend will always provide you with valid confluence areas like the ones shown in the above charts. When situations like the abovementioned occur, the trend is about to end usually.

Think of the confluence area as a goldilocks zone, the area where you will find the best trading setups possible, each with great chances of success.

Thinks of the confluence area as a descending triangle for a downtrend and an ascending one for an uptrend.

REJECTION CONFIRMATION

Okay, thus far you have learned how to find meaningful support and resistance areas on a higher timeframe to filter out the bad trades. You've learned the best methods to analyze price action trends and develop confluence areas where you are expecting price to reach. Now what?

As it is now, the trading strategy is not complete. You can't just enter a trade when price reaches your confluence area and hope for the best. You need confirmation from price action movements that the trend will indeed resume after reaching the confluence zone. In other words, you need to see how price behaves when it finally reaches the confluence area. You need to see if there are enough orders there to change the momentum and reverse price direction, resuming the trend. If there are, price action movements will give you plenty of signs, you just need to train your eye in order to spot them. From now on I am going to call this whole concept "Rejection". It is a rejection of a price area, the rejection of our confluence zone.

PRICE ACTION SIGNS OF REJECTION

There are a number of clues the market will give you that there are sizable orders in the confluence area, in the direction of the trend. I am now going to name the most powerful signs of rejection we are going to use to judge if price is rejecting the confluence area.

1. Price spikes or candlestick wicks
2. Impulsive moves change direction
3. Big directional candles change direction
4. Price starts to move sideways
5. Price stops making HH's or LL's

CHART 19: LOOKING FOR REJECTION SIGNS

Let's break down the chart above.

We have an uptrend, price is making higher highs and higher lows.

We have 2 congestion areas of roughly the same size.

We develop the confluence area. It looks like an ascending triangle. So far so good.

If you want, you can plot the Fibonacci retracement tool on the last impulsive move of the downtrend to see if the 50% and/or 61.8% retracement levels are inside the confluence area. The last impulsive move starts at the last HL and ends at point A.

This is the 4h chart. Price has gone all the way up to point A and is starting to retrace. You are watching it making its way down, inside the confluence area.

At this point, in order to see the rejection signs, we need to go down to a smaller timeframe to see all the small movements price is starting to make once inside the confluence area.

The 15 minutes timeframe always seems to do the trick. It's low enough to see all the minor price action movements in detail and, at the same time, high enough to hide all the intraday noise and erratic movements price makes. We are going to concentrate on the retracement move of the 4h uptrend. That is the move from point A to point B.

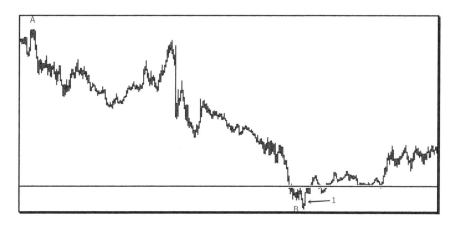

CHART 20: PRICE SPIKES AND SIDEWAYS MOVEMENT

This is the same chart but a different timeframe. The 15m. The down move from point A to point B is the retracement move against the main trend on the 4h chart. On this low timeframe there is a different perspective. The A->B move is actually the current trend on this timeframe. You analyze it just like you would any other trend, looking for clues of rejection. The horizontal line is the boundary of the confluence area on the 4h chart.

The short move down marked with "1" is a price spike. It protrudes away from surrounding price, goes down fast and comes back up again, just as fast. It looks like the letter "V". What could have caused such price behavior in the confluence area there? Yes, you guessed it. Buyers felt price has gone low enough for them to enter the market.

After the price spike you can see small swings inside other swings. This is sideways movement. Another signal that the retracement (downtrend on the 15m) is about to end. You come to this conclusion by analyzing the whole retracement move from point A to point B. From the top you can see price making LH's and LL's. Then, when it hits the confluence area, after the spike, it fails to make additional LL's and starts to move sideways.

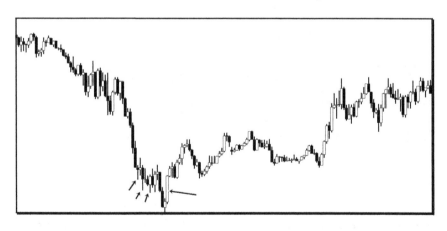

CHART 21: CANDLE WICKS AND BIG DIRECTIONAL CANDLES

This is the same exact chart and the same 15m timeframe but with candlesticks instead of bars. See the zone with the price spike there at the bottom. Look at how, when price enters the confluence area, the candles starts to develop wicks on the downside. This is emphasized by the 3 small arrows on the left side of the spike. To give this the importance it deserves, again, you need to judge it into the right context.

Notice the whole down move from the top and observe how there are barely any candle wicks at all. Only when price encounters the confluence area, it starts to reject it. The wicks on the downside show rejection of that price area, they show buyers entering the market.

Next, observe the price spike, this time with candlesticks. Notice that big white directional candle that pushed the price up very fast and developed the spike. Put it into context. Do you see a similar white candle in the whole retracement move, up until that point? No, there isn't. There were only big black directional candles. This too is a sign that the main trend on the 4h might resume.

CHART 22: DOWNTREND REJECTION ANALYSIS

On this chart we have the same situation like in the one above but in the other direction. There is a downtrend, you find the confluence area and wait for price to start retrace from point A where it currently is.

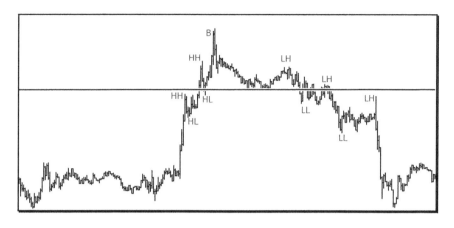

CHART 23: RETRACEMENT MOVE STOPS MAKING HH'S AND HL'S

This is the same chart but on the 15m timeframe. See how the upwards retracement move that ends at point B, inside the confluence area, fails to make any additional HH's and HL's when in retraces inside the confluence zone. The small uptrend on the 15m behaves normally until it encounters the confluence area. Then it starts to exhibit signs of exhaustion. The sellers feel price has gone high enough and jump into the market to resume the downtrend.

Just as with the first example, there is a price spike there, that looks like an inverted "V", at point B there on the higher area in the middle of the chart.

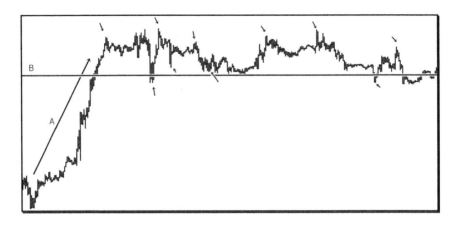

CHART 24: MARKET TURNING IN SIDEWAYS MOTION WHEN CONFLUENCE AREA REACHED

Here is another example of how price behaves when the retracement move reaches the confluence area. There is a downtrend in place, price is retracing upwards towards the confluence area. Move "A" is the retracement move, Line "B" is the boundary of the confluence area, or the horizontal line of the descending triangle, however you want to think of it. Prior to reaching into the confluence area, price has no problem moving upwards as you can see. It goes up fast without any trouble, no swings, no meaningful congestion areas, no typical back and forth movement. The retracement is forceful.

As you can see, once inside the confluence area, things change quite a bit. Price encounters selling orders and starts to move sideways. There are many swings inside other swings there. The buyers fail to push the price further up past all the barriers in the confluence area. Another strong sign that price is rejecting the confluence area and the trend will most likely resume.

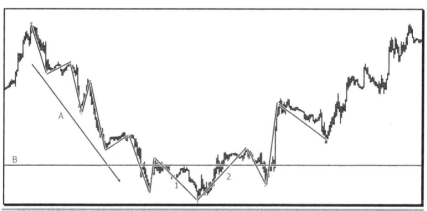

CHART 25: IMPULSIVE MOVES CHANGE DIRECTION WHEN CONFLUENCE AREA REACHED

See this example of price behavior inside the confluence area. There is an uptrend in place on the 4h chart. This is a 15m chart of course. The "A" move is the retracement towards the confluence area. The "B" line is the boundary of the confluence area. As far as this 15m timeframe is concerned, the down move "A" that we call a retracement of the 4h uptrend is the actual trend here. You can see how price is making LL's and LH's on the left of the chart. You can also see impulsive and retracement moves of this 15m trend marked with lines on top of price. That is a textbook downtrend.

But see what happens when price goes low enough to reach the confluence area. Move "1", the last impulsive move of the 15m downtrend (which is, again, the retracement of the 4h uptrend) is not followed by another retracement. Move "2" happens instead, an impulsive move but in the opposite direction. From there on you can see price making HH's and HL's. The 15m downtrend has clearly ended and the 4h uptrend has clearly resumed.

Another price action sign that you will find from time to time, when the sideways movement becomes large enough, is price rotations getting smaller and smaller inside the confluence area. This means a break away from the area is imminent.

Depending on what market you are trading, if available, the trading volume can be used also in your rejection of confluence area analysis. If you are trading a market where the total trading volume is centralized, it will be available on your charting platform. Basically, a price move, accompanied by high volume is a clear indication that new orders have been entered into the market and that move is a meaningful one. A price move without the company of higher than normal trading volume can be a short spike. You can use volume in your big directional bar changing direction analysis for example. If inside the confluence area you get big directional bars appearing in the direction of the main trend, you can look at the volume to see if this too confirms what you are seeing on the chart. You can use volume to judge the solidity of new impulsive moves inside the confluence area. If you get an impulsive move in the direction of the main trend, you already know this means a rejection of the confluence area, but you get further confirmation when you see the move accompanied by high volume.

Another suggestion to take a break from reading at this point.

Go to the charts, and get accustomed to how price behaves when it reaches the confluence area. Study those same trends you already did practice on, go to the 15m timeframes in order to zoom in on the price movements inside the confluence zones.

See if you can find the price action signs of rejection discussed above

Do that until you have enough information to draw your own conclusions.

You don't need to find all the signs in each confluence area. You won't. The important thing is to train your eye to see this behavior of price and easily recognize it when trading. If you can find at least two distinct signs in each confluence area that is good enough.

See what happens if you can't find any signs at all. Does the trend resume in such cases?

ACT on IT

There is one more thing you need to do in order to have a complete trading plan. So far what you have done is this:

1. Identify support and resistance on daily timeframe
2. Identify price action trend on 4h timeframe
3. Develop confluence area
4. Observe rejection of confluence area on the 15m timeframe

It is now time to put all the knowledge to work. It is time to define the exact trade entry along with finding a place for the protective stop. As you have seen from previous chart examples throughout the book, when the retracement movement reaches the confluence area 2 things are most likely to happen. One is price making a sharp spike that goes away from the surrounding price territory. This is the "V" or inverted V move price movement that you've seen in many of the chart examples. Some decent in amplitude, some smaller, some bigger but a price spike nevertheless. A second scenario that you may have noticed by studying the charts is price starting to move sideways, making price swings inside other swings.

Either way, you will need to pin point the exact price level where you are going to enter the trade, and the place for the protective stop. The profit target will be a conservative one, always in the area of the last LL of a downtrend or at the last HH of an uptrend. You don't want to get greedy in trading.

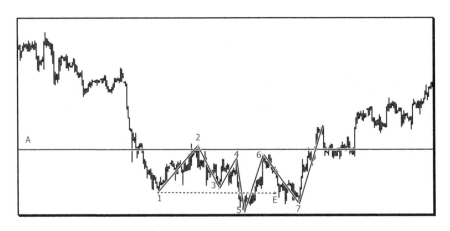

CHART 26: PATTERN TO DEFINE ENTRY

See the above chart.

There is an uptrend on the 4h chart. Price is retracing downwards.

The A line is the boundary of the confluence area. This is the 15m chart.

Price has reached the confluence area,

At this point you need to wait for the first price swing inside the confluence area. The 1->2 move gives you that. This initial 1 to 2 move will be used to define the entry. The entry will always be at the extension of swing "1". You can see the extension on the chart marked with that dotted horizontal arrow. At the end of the arrow at point "E" is where the trade will be entered. So you will need to wait for the 6 to 7 move to reach the swing 1 price level territory, coming from the upside in order to enter the trade.

Why not enter when the 4 to 5 move reached the

extension of swing 1?

This is a pattern that works time and time again. The idea behind it is the following. The initial 1-2 move has to be surpassed in either direction before you can expect for price to touch swing 1 territory and enter the trade.

It is a simple 3 steps process

Wait for the first swing, or the first move in line with the main trend, after price has reached inside the confluence area, In the above example this is the 1-2 move.

Wait for this initial 1-2 move to be surpassed in either direction. In the above chart, it is the 4 to 5 move that goes below the 1-2 territory.

Finally, after the move that surpassed the territory of the initial move, wait for price to reach the extension of the first swing inside the confluence area. In the chart above, that is "E".

The protective stop will always be set above or below the move that surpassed the initial one. In the above chart, the stop will be set below the "5" swing.

What is the meaning of this entry criteria?

It is all about support and resistance, all about the war between the buyers and sellers. They create predictable patterns in the market.

Look at it this way. After the 1-2 move inside the confluence area, we can safely say that we have buyers at point 1 and we have sellers at point 2. Right? It is more than obvious. We can see it. Otherwise price wouldn't have changed direction the way it did at these points in the market. This creates support at point 1 and resistance for price at point 2. You already know that everyone wants to enter the market at an advantageous price. Well, swing 5 is considered very good by the buyers. They bought at "1" earlier which was at a higher price level, they bought at "3" which was even higher. They see that "5" like the perfect opportunity to enter the market and continue the uptrend. The idea is that the lower price goes, the more buyers it will attract.

Price goes to 6, finds sellers there, it can't resume the uptrend just yet, it needs more buyers. The perfect place to find those extra buyers is at the support in the area of swing 1, where it found them before. The idea behind it is that most of the times, big upwards moves start from a strong support, where the market triggers enough buying orders. Conversely with a big downwards move. The market must go to a strong resistance zone to find enough sellers before it can go down.

CHART 27: DOWNTREND DEFINING ENTRY LEVEL

Here is the same scenario but with a downtrend in the 4h chart.

Price enters the confluence area delimited by the horizontal line across the whole chart. Makes the initial 1 to 2 move that immediately gets surpassed on the upside at swing 3. Entry happens the after price goes to 4 and retraces back to the extension of swing 1. The entry is marked on the chart with a circle. This is an even clearer pattern then the one in the first example. Price going at 3, attracts more sellers, price going at 4 attracts buyers, price revisiting the area of swing 1 which is now resistance for price, attracts enough sellers to resume the trend. The higher price goes, the more sellers it finds. The more sellers or selling volume it finds, the more chances for the downtrend to break through support barriers and resume.

Why did the market's back and forth rotations attracted more sellers on the upside than buyers on the downside swings? Because the main trend, the one on the 4h chart of this security is pointing down. Its only logical that there will be more people interested in selling in a downtrend that there would be interested in buying.

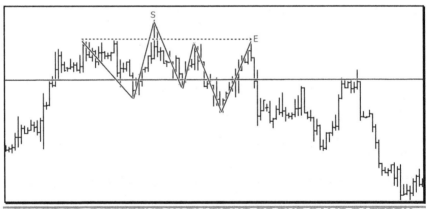

CHART 28: DIFFERENT VARIATIONS OF THE SAME PATTERN

You can see the same thing happening here, only that the pattern is more developed then the previous. The principle behind it is the same though.

Downtrend on 4h, price inside confluence area, initial move gets broken to the upside at point S (S is where the protective stop of the trade will be). Eventually after it goes down, price need to attract more sellers to resume the trend. It goes up looking for them at point E (the entry of the trade).

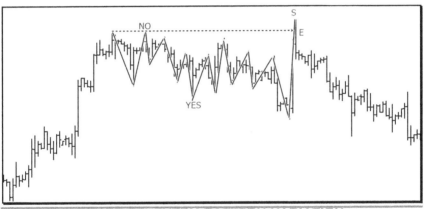

CHART 29: ENTRY PATTERN VARIATION

Here is a slightly different pattern than the above ones. The difference is that the break of the first initial move happens to the downside in a downtrend at the "yes" swing there. The "no" swing is not really a break of the initial move. You need to see a break away from the initial move territory. Price has to move convincingly past it. Remember that this is not exact science so there are no precise measurements to what constitutes a convincingly and a not so convincingly move. But, if you are having trouble seeing with the naked eye if a move has gone above or below the initial move then it sure doesn't count as a break. It has to be clear with the naked eye immediately. In this scenario, you sell when point E is reached, after the "yes" swing happens. The stop loss will be where the upwards move stops.

What does breaking the initial move to the downside in a downtrend mean? It means that the buyers are weak. They don't even have the power to even try and challenge the sellers by going above the initial move. In such situations where the initial move is broken at the "yes" swing, there is an advantageous price level for them to buy there, but even so, they can't manage to challenge the sellers by piercing through the resistance. Only when price goes further down at a second try, it sparks enough buying interest to push the price to point E.

Buyers failing to challenge the sellers means they are not convinced the current price area is a good opportunity for them. The market needs to go lower to find balance between buyers and sellers. And it does.

If at any moment when trying to distinguish the price swings that compose the entry pattern seem way too erratic to you, it seems too hard to decide, feel free to move to a clearer timeframe, that reduces all the noise but still shows all the minor swings you need to see in order to find the entry level.

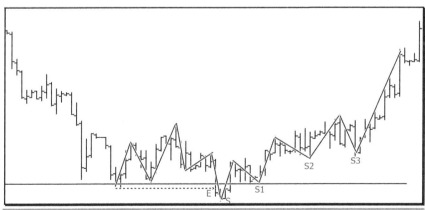

CHART 30: VARIATION IN UPTREND

See this chart above. The same thing is happening as with the previous example. The difference is that the trend on the 4h is pointing upwards. The break of the initial move happens to the upside. See the entry, the initial place of the protective stop and how you will trail that stop into profit, as the trade starts to go in favor.

S1, S2, S3, are perfect areas to trail the stop loss into profit because they are derived from the minor price action trend. They are not random levels in the market. They are the HL's of the small uptrend price makes on its way to your take profit level.

The first type setups however, where the break of the initial move happens to the downside in an uptrend and to the upside in a downtrend are more common. See your past charts and get used to both types of setups. Practice with them until you get comfortable.

The take profit is, as said before, at the beginning of the retracement move on the 4h chart.

Usually, with this type of trades, the risk reward ratio is 1 to 2 at least, more often than not even 1 to 3.

Go to your charts, practice, demo trade until you feel confident enough in your skills.

Find the setup, wait for the entry, manage the trade, repeat.

MANAGE THE RISK

As you might have noticed from the above trade examples, the strategy is manufactured in such a way that every single trade provides low risk and high reward. Regardless of what trading strategy you use, you must always look to reduce your risk as much as possible and maximize the profits. This way you can come out as profitable even if you lose more trades then you win. Before entering any trade, you must already know what you will be risking to lose if the trade goes bad. This should be your main concern. Look at price action, see where your protective stop should be and then look to see where your profit target is. If the potential profit is not at least 1.5-2 times greater than the risk you will be taking, then discard the trade. Wait for a better opportunity.

No matter how good the potential trade looks like, if it doesn't meet the criteria with respect to risk-reward ratio, do not take the trade. If there are occasions when the risk in absolute value is too much for you to take even if the potential reward is 3 times larger, reduce the order size to a level where you feel comfortable with the potential loss if the trade goes bad.

After entry, always manage the trade, don't leave the stop in the initial place after the trade starts going into profit. Try to protect what you have earned without compromising the trade. Set the protective stop into profit but at a distance from the current price. Always use price action logical levels to move your stops into profit territory. The stop must be in a place where current price has the least chances of getting at. A place where, if reached, it will invalidate the logic and analysis of the whole trade. This will ensure that you give enough space for the trade to develop and eventually reach your target.

Let the profits run. Once you've decided where the take profit must be, don't change it. Let the trade develop. Don't close the trade early, in fear that price will reverse and hit your stop.

Depending on the market you are trading, pay attention to volatility. Don't set the stop level exactly above or below. Think of it as an area rather than an exact point. This will allow room for random price spikes to develop without hitting your protective stops.

PATIENCE AND DISCIPLINE

These are key to any trader looking to become consistently profitable and eventually make a living out of trading the markets. The trading strategy presented in this book is very solid and will provide great results over time. However, it is of zero value to you if you don't learn discipline.

Don't ever bend the rules thinking it will work just as well. It won't.

Don't get greedy. No matter how good the trade setup looks, stick to your rules and your predetermined order size.

Trading can get boring. There are many times when nothing is happening in the market. Trading requires work. Have patience and wait for the best setups only, just like those presented throughout the book.

No matter what strategy you use, you will always have bad trades from time to time. Don't let your emotions cloud your judgement. Take the loss and move on. Very soon you will get the chance to recuperate that loss many times over.

Every loss should be a lesson to learn from. Study what happened, identify what mistake you've made, write it down and try not to do it again.

There will be occasions where you don't do anything wrong but still suffer a small loss. This is part of trading. Don't try to explain what cannot be explained. The market makes random moves occasionally. The strategy is not bad. Don't change it. Stick to it and always manage the risk.

CLOSING WORDS

The strategy presented is derived from years of experience in the market. It has all that you need to become a profitable trader month after month. All you need to do is make sure you understand correctly all that is presented. Read the book as many times as it takes, do the practice sessions on your charts, test it on your demo account before putting your own money into it. Let the information sink in. My experience is that not everyone looking to become a good trader has the analytical nature required to put to work a strategy designed to pay attention to details. Read it, read it again, practice and decide if it is for you or not. Be honest with yourself.

If you are inclined to trade with even higher timeframes then the ones used by me, feel free to use the daily charts as the main timeframe. The weekly for the support and resistance above and below current price. Use the 1h timeframe for the rejection of the confluence area analysis. It will be just as efficient.

I do not recommend going on lower timeframes than the ones I use. As with any trading strategy, the lower the timeframes, the less reliable it becomes. If you must, test it first over a set period and see what results you come up with. If they are satisfactory, please go ahead and use it. The concepts that build the strategy are sound and proven to work over time. They are valid regardless of the timeframe used. Erratic intraday price movements are what you will have to pay close attention to.

Suggested complementary reading: Price Action Breakdown by Laurentiu Damir

At this point I feel that I've done a pretty thorough explanation of the trading strategy and price action concepts involved in it. If there are some aspects of the book that need further clarification the email is readtheprice@gmail.com. As free time is limited, I would very much appreciate you taking 1 minute of your time to write a review of the book on Amazon. If I am going to spend time answering questions, it seems only fair that you take a minute of your time to post a few words on amazon :)